FINGERPICKING HYMNS

INTRODUCTION TO FINGERSTYLE GUITAR   2

ABIDE WITH ME   6
AMAZING GRACE   8
BE THOU MY VISION   10
BENEATH THE CROSS OF JESUS   12
BLESSED ASSURANCE   3
COME, THOU FOUNT OF EVERY BLESSING   14
FAIREST LORD JESUS   16
FOOTSTEPS OF JESUS   18
FOR THE BEAUTY OF THE EARTH   20
HOLY, HOLY, HOLY! LORD GOD ALMIGHTY   22
I'VE GOT PEACE LIKE A RIVER   24
IN THE GARDEN   26
JACOB'S LADDER   32
A MIGHTY FORTRESS IS OUR GOD   28
ROCK OF AGES   30

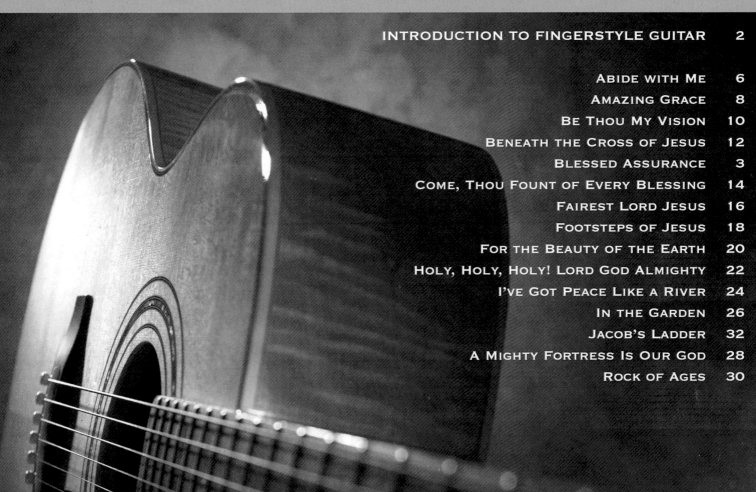

ISBN 978-0-634-09343-2

Copyright © 2005
by HAL LEONARD CORPORATION
International Copyright Secured
All Rights Reserved

In Australia Contact:
Hal Leonard Australia Pty. Ltd.
4 Lentara Court
Cheltenham, Victoria, 3192 Australia
Email: ausadmin@halleonard.com

Visit Hal Leonard Online at
www.halleonard.com

HAL•LEONARD®
CORPORATION
7777 W. BLUEMOUND RD. P.O. BOX 13819 MILWAUKEE, WI 53213

INTRODUCTION TO FINGERSTYLE GUITAR

Fingerstyle (a.k.a. fingerpicking) is a guitar technique that means you literally pick the strings with your right-hand fingers and thumb. This contrasts with the conventional technique of strumming and playing single notes with a pick (a.k.a. flatpicking). For fingerpicking, you can use any type of guitar: acoustic steel-string, nylon-string classical, or electric.

THE RIGHT HAND

The most common right-hand position is shown here.

Use a high wrist; arch your palm as if you were holding a ping-pong ball. Keep the thumb outside and away from the fingers, and let the fingers do the work rather than lifting your whole hand.

The thumb generally plucks the bottom strings with downstrokes on the left side of the thumb and thumbnail. The other fingers pluck the higher strings using upstrokes with the fleshy tip of the fingers and fingernails. The thumb and fingers should pluck one string per stroke and not brush over several strings.

Another picking option you may choose to use is called hybrid picking (a.k.a. plectrum-style fingerpicking). Here, the pick is usually held between the thumb and first finger, and the three remaining fingers are assigned to pluck the higher strings.

THE LEFT HAND

The left-hand fingers are numbered 1 through 4.

Be sure to keep your fingers arched, with each joint bent; if they flatten out across the strings, they will deaden the sound when you fingerpick. As a general rule, let the strings ring as long as possible when playing fingerstyle.

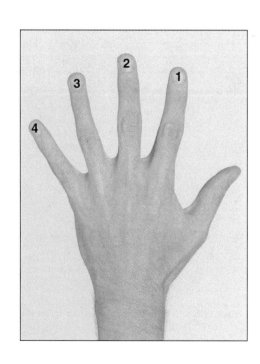

Blessed Assurance

Lyrics by Fanny J. Crosby
Music by Phoebe Palmer Knapp

1. Bles - sed as - sur - ance, Je - sus is mine! _____
2., 3. *See additional lyrics*

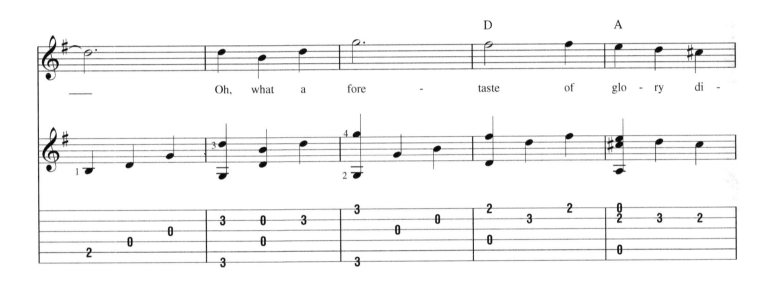

_____ Oh, what a fore - taste of glo - ry di -

vine! _____ Heir of sal - va - tion,

Chorus

pur - chase of God, _____ born of His spir -
it, _____ washed in His blood. _____ This is my
sto - ry, this is my song, _____
prais - ing my Sav - ior all the day long. _____

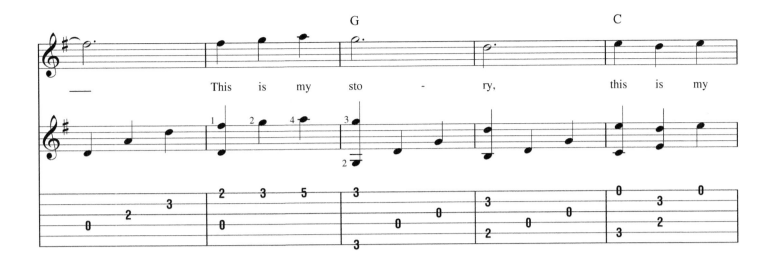

This is my sto - ry, this is my

song, _____ prais - ing my Sav - ior

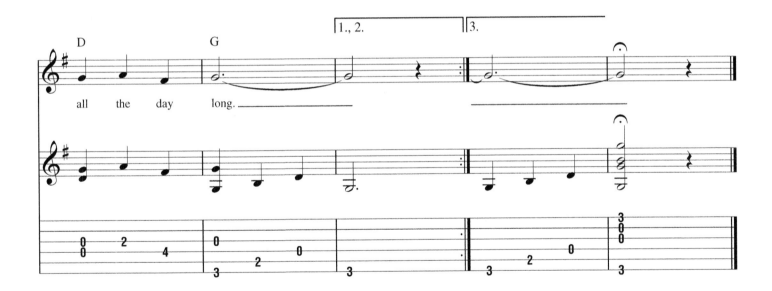

all the day long. _____

Additional Lyrics

2. Perfect submission, perfect delight,
   Visions of rapture now burst on my sight;
   Angels descending, bring from above
   Echoes of mercy, whispers of love.

3. Perfect submission, all is at rest.
   I in my Savior am happy and blest,
   Watching and waiting, looking above,
   Filled with His goodness, lost in His love.

Abide with Me

Words by Henry F. Lyte
Music by William H. Monk

1. A - bide with me; fast falls the e - ven tide.
2. - 5. *See additional lyrics*

The dark - ness deep - ens; Lord, with me a - bide!

When oth - er help - ers fail and com - forts

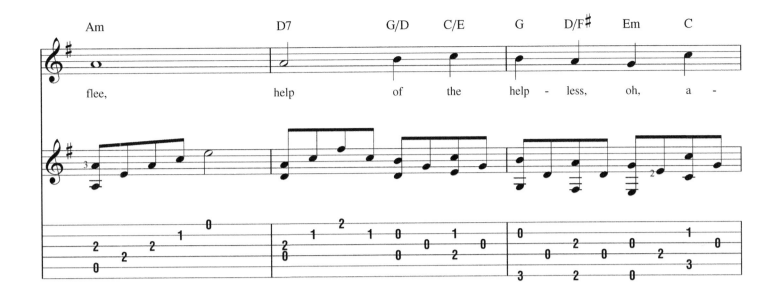

Additional Lyrics

2. Swift to its close ebbs out life's little day.
   Earth's joys grow dim; its glories pass away.
   Change and decay in all around I see.
   Oh, Thou who changest not, abide with me.

3. I need Thy presence every passing hour;
   What but Thy grace can foil the tempter's power?
   Who, like thyself, my guide and stay can be?
   Through cloud and sunshine, Lord, abide with me.

4. I fear no foe, with Thee at hand to bless.
   Ills have no weight, and tears not bitterness.
   Where is death's sting? Where, grave, thy victory?
   I triumph still if Thou abide with me.

5. Hold Thou Thy cross before my closing eyes;
   Shine through the gloom and point me to to the skies.
   Heav'n's morning breaks, and earth's vain shadows flee;
   In life, in death, oh Lord, abide with me.

Amazing Grace

Words by John Newton
From A Collection of Sacred Ballads
Traditional American Melody
From Carrell and Clayton's Virginia Harmony

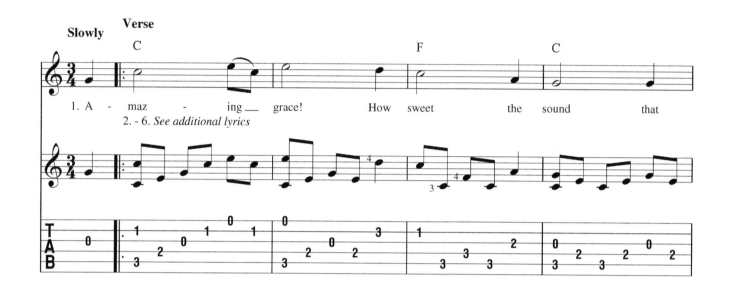

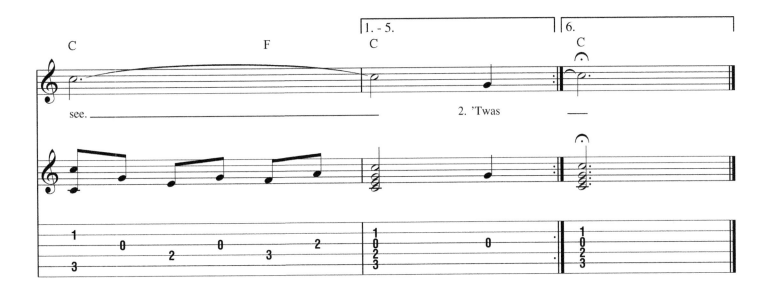

Additional Lyrics

2. 'Twas grace that taught my heart to fear,
   And grace my fears relieved.
   How precious did that grace appear
   The hour I first believed.

3. Through many dangers, toils and snares
   I have already come.
   'Tis grace hath brought me safe thus far
   And grace will lead me home.

4. The Lord has promised good to me,
   His word my hope secures.
   He will my shield and portion be
   As long as life endures.

5. Yea, when this flesh and heart shall fail,
   And mortal life shall cease,
   I shall possess within the veil
   A life of joy and peace.

6. When we've been there ten thousand years,
   Bright shining as the sun,
   We've no less days to sing God's praise
   Than when we've first begun.

Be Thou My Vision

Traditional Irish
Translated by Mary E. Byrne

Drop D tuning:
(low to high) D-A-D-G-B-E

1. Be thou my ___ vi - sion, oh Lord of my
2., 3., 4. *See additional lyrics*

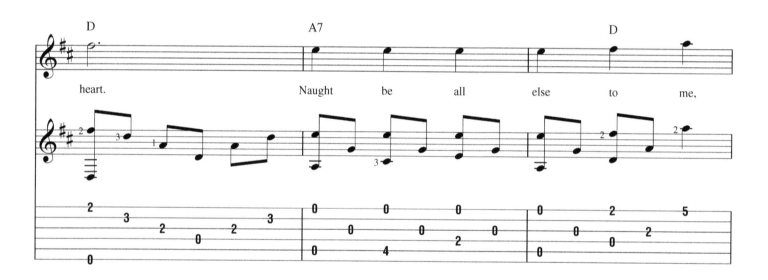

heart. Naught be all else to me,

save that Thou art. Thou my ___ best ___

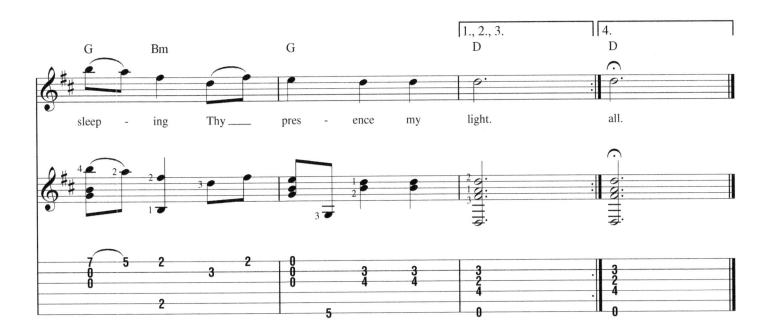

Additional Lyrics

2. Riches I heed not, nor man's empty praise.
   Thou mine inheritance, now and always.
   Thou and Thou only, first in my heart.
   High King of heaven, my treasure Thou art.

3. Be Thou my Wisdom, and Thou my true word;
   I ever with Thee and Thou with me, Lord.
   Thou my great Father, I Thy true son;
   Thou in me dwelling, and I with Thee one.

4. High King of heaven, my victory won.
   May I reach heaven's joys, O bright heav'n's sun!
   Heart of my own heart, whatever befall,
   Still be my Vision, O Ruler of all.

Beneath the Cross of Jesus

Words by Elizabeth Cecelia Douglas Clephane
Music by Frederick Charles Maker

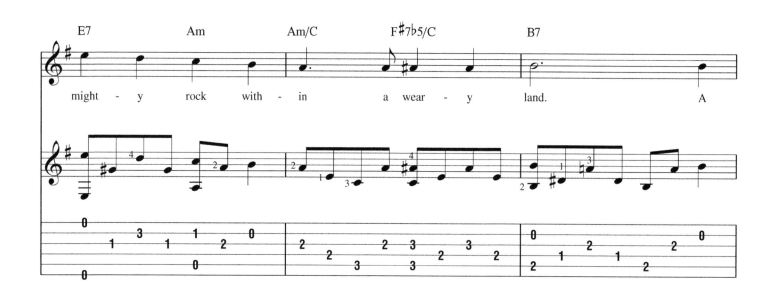

Additional Lyrics

2. Upon that cross of Jesus, mine eye at times can see
   The very dying form of One who suffered there for me.
   And from my stricken heart, with tears, two wonders I confess:
   The wonders of redeeming love and my unworthiness.

Come, Thou Fount of Every Blessing

Words by Robert Robinson
Music by The Sacred Harp

1. Come, Thou fount of ev'ry bles-sing, tune my heart to sing Thy
2., 3. *See additional lyrics*

grace. Streams of mer-cy, nev-er ceas-ing, call for songs of loud-est

praise. Teach me some mel-o-dious son-net, sung by flam-ing tongues a-

bove.   Praise   the   mount!   I'm   fixed   up - on   it,   mount   of

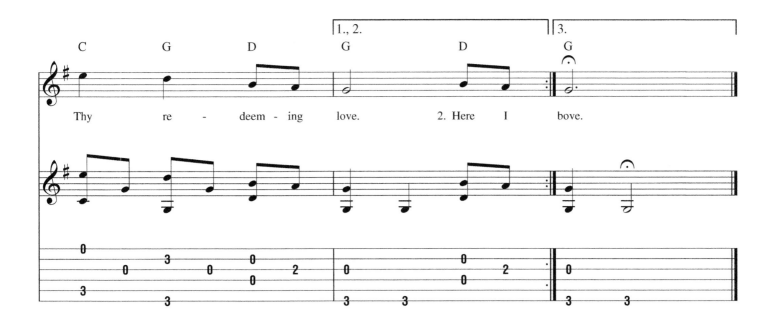

Thy   re - deem - ing love.   2. Here   I   bove.

Additional Lyrics

2. Here I raise mine Ebenezer,
   Hither by Thy help I'm come.
   And I hope, by Thy good pleasure,
   Safely to arrive at home.
   Jesus sought me when a stranger,
   Wand'ring from the fold of God;
   He, to rescue me from danger,
   Interposed His precious blood.

3. Oh, to grace how great a debtor
   Daily I'm constrained to be!
   Let Thy grace, Lord, like a fetter,
   Bind my wand'ring heart to Thee.
   Prone to wander, Lord I feel it,
   Prone to leave the God I love;
   Here's my heart, Lord, take and seal it,
   Seal it for Thy courts above.

Fairest Lord Jesus

Words from Munster Gesangbuch
Verse 4 by Joseph A. Seiss
Music from Schlesische Volkslieder

1. Fair - est Lord Je - sus, ru - ler of all
2., 3., 4. *See additional lyrics*

na - ture, oh, Thou of God and _____

man the son; Thee will I

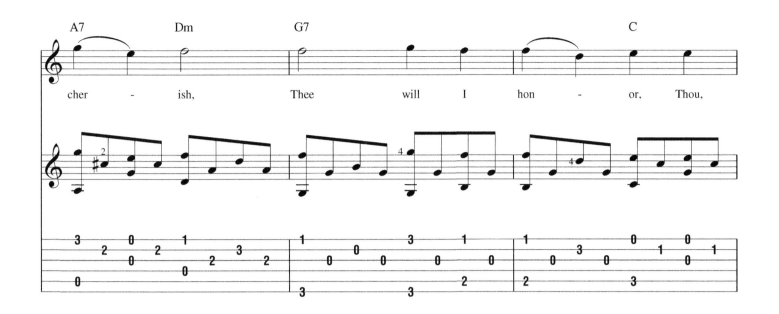

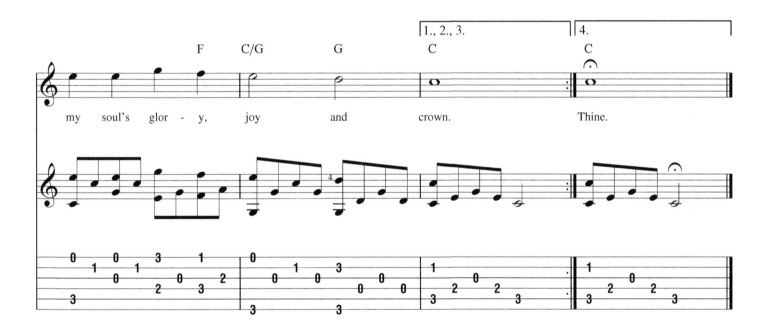

Additional Lyrics

2. Fair are the meadows, fairer still the woodlands,
   Robed in the blooming garb of spring.
   Jesus is fairer, Jesus is purer,
   Who makes the woeful heart to sing.

3. Fair is the sunshine, fairer still the moonlight,
   And all the twinkling, starry host.
   Jesus shines brighter, Jesus shines purer
   Than all the angels heaven can boast.

4. Beautiful Savior! Lord of the nations!
   Son of God and Son of Man!
   Glory and honor, praise, adoration
   Now and forevermore be Thine.

Footsteps of Jesus

Words by Mary B.C. Slade
Music by Asa B. Everett

1. Sweet - ly, Lord, have we heard Thee call - ing, "Come, fol - low
2., 3., 4. *See additional lyrics*

me!" And we see where Thy foot - prints fall - ing,

lead us to Thee. Foot - prints of

Je - sus that make the path - way glow;

we will fol - low the steps of Je - sus where - e'er they

1., 2., 3.

go.

4.

go.

Additional Lyrics

2. Though they lead o'er the cold, dark mountains,
   Seeking His sheep;
   Or along by Siloam's fountains,
   Helping the weak.

3. If they lead through the temple holy,
   Preaching the Word;
   Or in homes of the poor and lowly,
   Serving the Lord.

4. Then at last, when on high He sees us,
   Our journey done;
   We will rest where the steps of Jesus
   End at His throne.

For the Beauty of the Earth

Words by Folliot S. Pierpoint
Music by Conrad Kocher

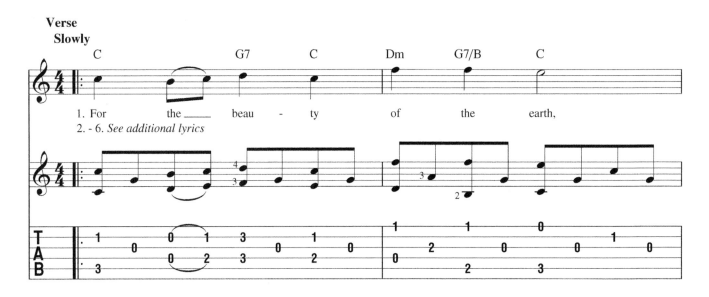

1. For the ___ beau-ty of the earth,
2. - 6. *See additional lyrics*

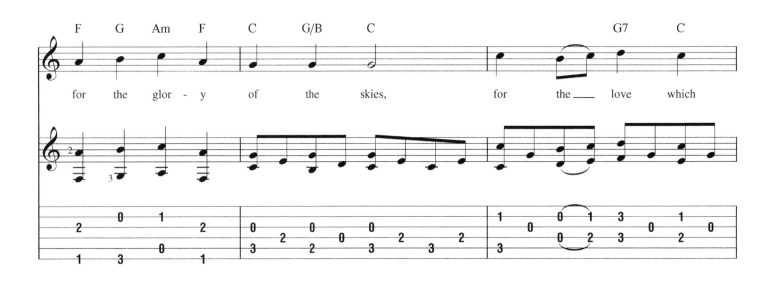

for the glo-ry of the skies, for the ___ love which

from our birth o-ver and a-round us lies,

Chorus

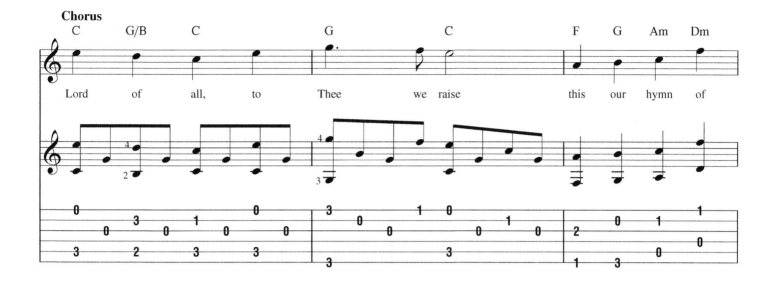

Lord of all, to Thee we raise this our hymn of

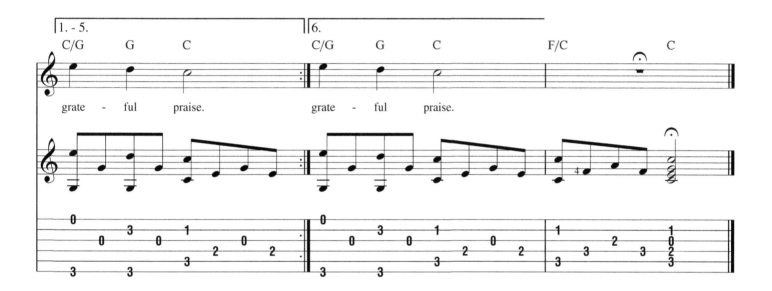

grate - ful praise. grate - ful praise.

Additional Lyrics

2. For the beauty of each hour,
   Of the day and of the night,
   Hill and vale, and tree and flower,
   Sun and moon and stars of light,

3. For the joy of ear and eye,
   For the heart and mind's delight,
   For the mystic harmony
   Linking sense to sound and sight,

4. For the joy of human love,
   Brother, sister, parent, child,
   Friends on earth and friends above,
   For all gentle thoughts and mild,

5. For Thy Church that evermore
   Lifteth holy hands above,
   Offering upon every shore
   Her pure sacrifice of love,

6. For Thy self, best Gift Divine,
   To the world so freely given,
   For that great, great love of Thine,
   Peace on earth and joy in heaven,

Holy, Holy, Holy! Lord God Almighty

Words by Reginald Heber
Music by John B. Dykes

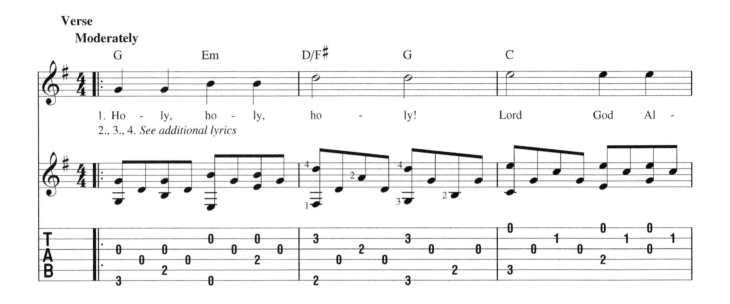

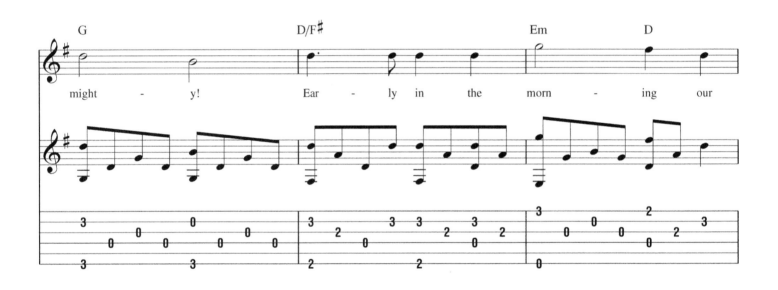

Additional Lyrics

2. Holy, holy, holy! All the saints adore Thee,
   Casting down their golden crowns around the glassy sea;
   Cherubim and seraphim falling down before Thee,
   Which wert and art and evermore shalt be.

3. Holy, holy, holy! Though the darkness hide Thee,
   Though the eye of sinful man Thy glory may not see.
   Only Thou art holy; there is none beside Thee,
   Perfect in power, in love, and purity.

4. Holy, holy, holy! Lord God Almighty!
   All Thy works shall praise Thy name in earth and sky and sea.
   Holy, holy, holy, merciful and mighty!
   God in three persons, blessed Trinity!

I've Got Peace Like a River

Traditional

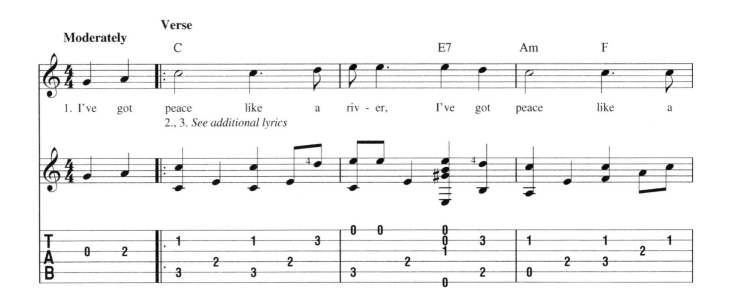

1. I've got peace like a river, I've got peace like a
2., 3. *See additional lyrics*

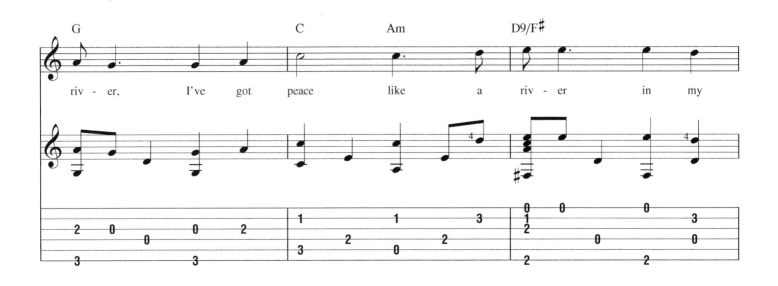

riv - er, I've got peace like a riv - er in my

soul. I've got peace like a

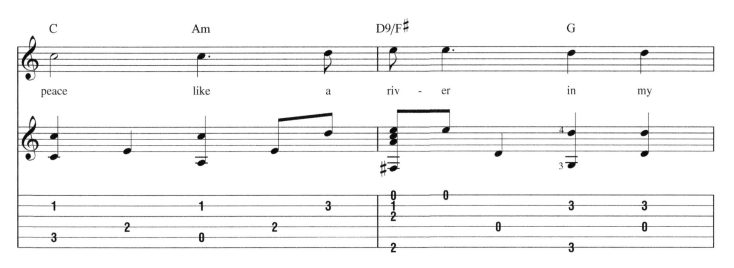

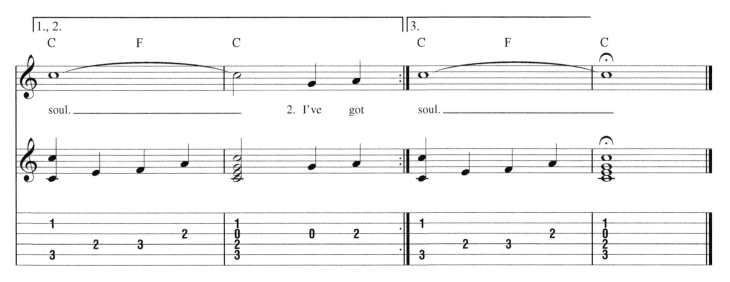

Additional Lyrics

2. I've got love like an ocean,
   I've got love like an ocean,
   I've got love like an ocean in my soul.
   I've got love like an ocean,
   I've got love like an ocean,
   I've got love like an ocean in my soul.

3. I've got joy like a fountain,
   I've got joy like a fountain,
   I've got joy like a fountain in my soul.
   I've got joy like a fountain,
   I've got joy like a fountain,
   I've got joy like a fountain in my soul.

In the Garden

Words and Music by C. Austin Miles

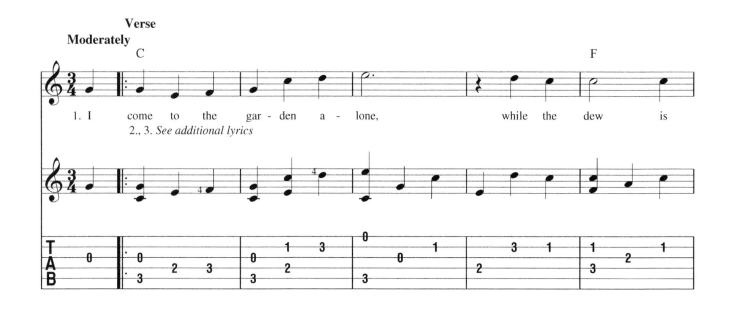

Chorus

walks with me and He talks with me, and He tells me I am His own, and the joy we share as we tar - ry there, none oth - er has ev - er known. _____ 2. He _____

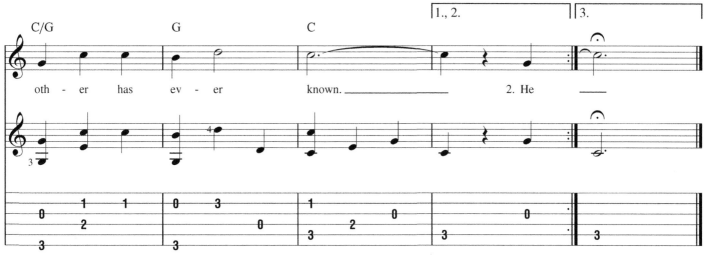

Additional Lyrics

2. He speaks, and the sound of His voice
   Is so sweet the birds hush their singing,
   And the melody that He gave to me
   Within my heart is ringing.

3. I'd stay in the garden with Him
   Though the night around me be falling,
   But He bids me go; through the voice of woe
   His voice to me is calling.

A Mighty Fortress Is Our God

Words and Music by Martin Luther
Translated by Frederick H. Hedge
Based on Psalm 46

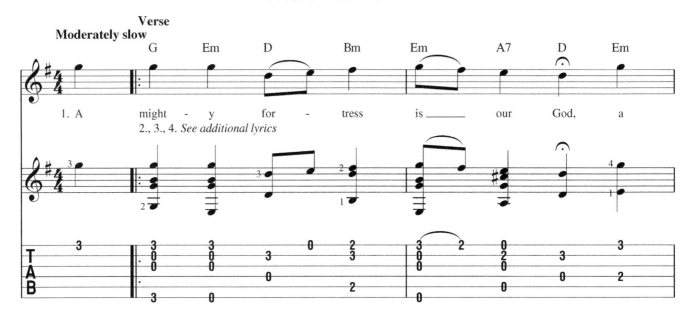

Verse
Moderately slow

1. A might - y for - tress is _____ our God, a
2., 3., 4. *See additional lyrics*

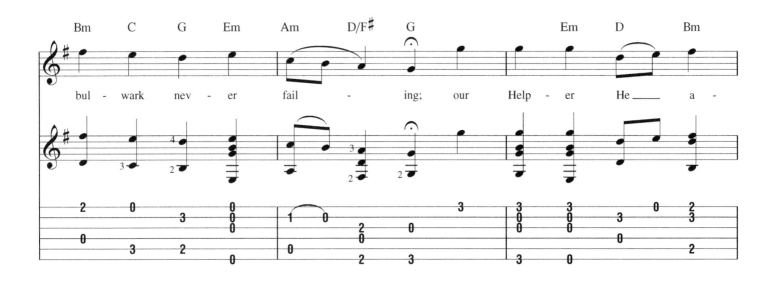

bul - wark nev - er fail - ing; our Help - er He _____ a -

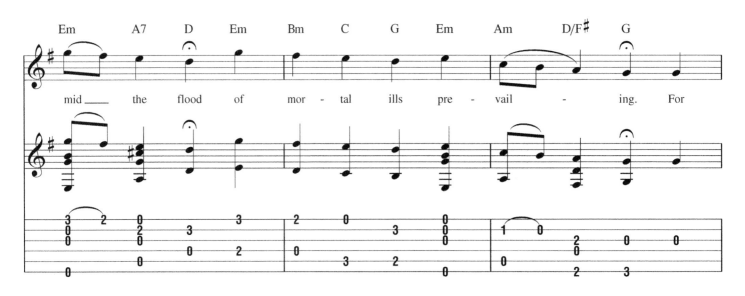

mid _____ the flood of mor - tal ills pre - vail - ing. For

Additional Lyrics

2. Did we in our own strength confide,
   Our striving would be losing,
   Were not the right man on our side,
   The man of God's own choosing.
   Dost ask who that may be?
   Christ Jesus, it is he;
   Lord Sabaoth, His name,
   From age to age the same,
   And He must win the battle.

3. And tho this world, with devils filled,
   Should threaten to undo us,
   We will not fear, for God hath willed
   His truth to triumph thru us.
   The prince of darkness grim,
   We tremble not for him;
   His rage we can endure,
   For lo, his doom is sure:
   One little word shall fell him.

4. That word above all earthly pow'rs,
   No thanks to them, abideth;
   The Spirit and the gifts are ours
   Thru Him who with us sideth.
   Let goods and kindred go,
   This mortal life also.
   The body they may kill;
   God's truth abideth still:
   His kingdom is forever.

Rock of Ages

Words by Augustus M. Toplady
V.1,2,4 altered by Thomas Cotterill
Music by Thomas Hastings

1. Rock of A - ges, cleft for me, let me hide my - self in
2., 3., 4. *See additional lyrics*

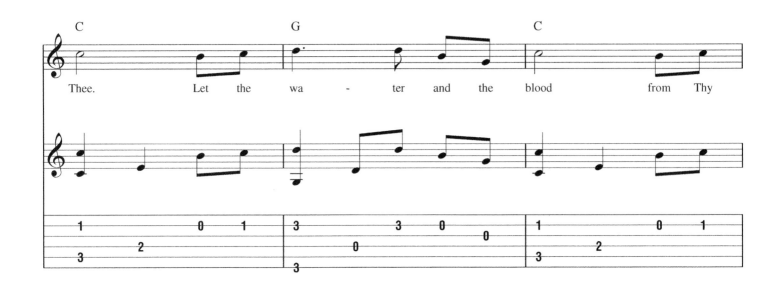

Thee. Let the wa - ter and the blood from Thy

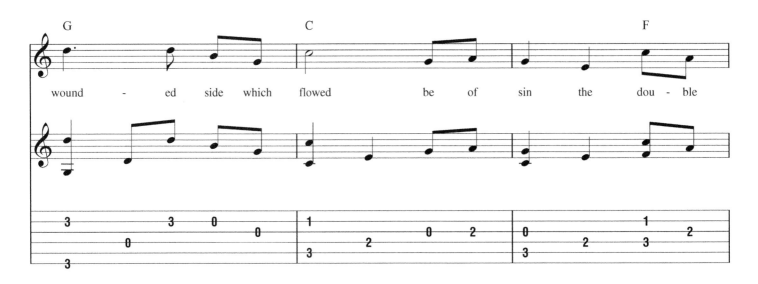

wound - ed side which flowed be of sin the dou - ble

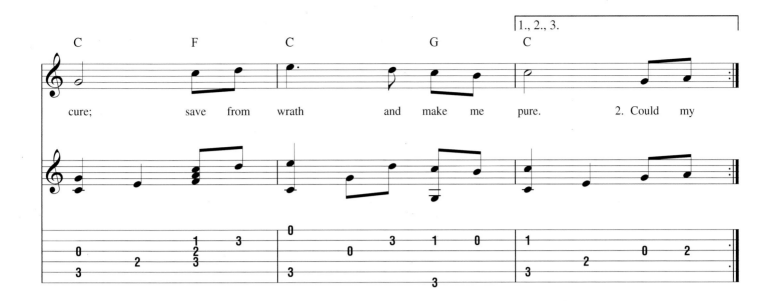

Additional Lyrics

2. Could my tears forever flow,
   Could my zeal no languor know?
   These for sin could not atone,
   Thou must save and Thou alone.
   I my hand no price I bring,
   Simply to Thy cross I cling.

3. Nothing in my hand I bring,
   Simply to the cross I cling.
   Naked, come to Thee for dress;
   Helpless, look to Thee for grace.
   Foul, I to the fountain fly;
   Wash me, Savior, or I die.

4. While I draw this fleeting breath,
   When my eyes shall close in death.
   When I rise to worlds unknown,
   And behold Thee on Thy throne.
   Rock of Ages, cleft for me,
   Let me hide myself in Thee,
   Let me hide myself in Thee.

Jacob's Ladder

African-American Spiritual

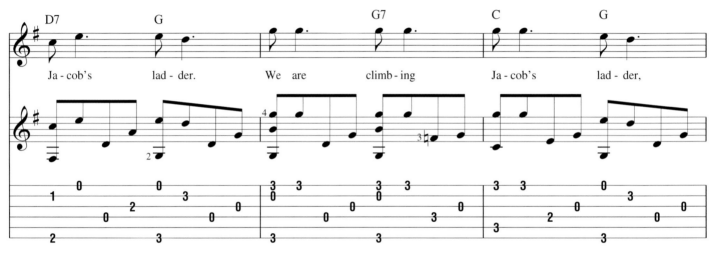

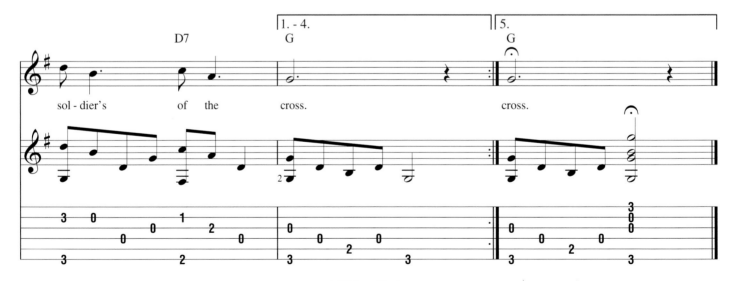

Additional Lyrics

2. Every round goes higher, higher,
   Every round goes higher, higher,
   Every round goes higher, higher,
   Soldiers of the cross.

3. Sinner, do you love my Jesus?
   Sinner, do you love my Jesus?
   Sinner, do you love my Jesus?
   Soldiers of the cross.

4. If you love Him, why not serve Him?
   If you love Him, why not serve Him?
   If you love Him, why not serve Him?
   Soldiers of the cross.

5. We are climbing higher, higher.
   We are climbing higher, higher.
   We are climbing higher, higher.
   Soldiers of the cross.